And the Beat Don't Stop

The views expressed in this work are solely those of the author and do not necessarily reflect the views of the publisher, and the publisher hereby disclaims any responsibility for them.

iUniverse books may be ordered through booksellers or by contacting:

iUniverse
1663 Liberty Drive
Bloomington, IN 47403
www.iuniverse.com
1-800-Authors (1-800-288-4677)

Because of the dynamic nature of the Internet, any web addresses or links contained in this book may have changed since publication and may no longer be valid.

Any people depicted in stock imagery provided by Thinkstock are models, and such images are being used for illustrative purposes only.

Certain stock imagery © Thinkstock.

ISBN: 978-1-4502-9175-0 (sc)
ISBN: 978-1-4502-9177-4 (dj)
ISBN: 978-1-4502-9176-7 (ebk)

Library of Congress Control Number: 2011901155

Printed in the United States of America

iUniverse rev. date: 5/4/2011

And

the

Beat

Don't

Stop

Jabreel Morgan

iUniverse, Inc.
Bloomington

Contents

EPIGRAPH

"Come, walk along the shores of my mind, leave your impression in the sand..."

Jabreel Morgan

PREFACE

Another baby was killed last night and the galaxies moan. I don't think it was time for this young child to return to its heavenly home. The Bible says we are born and the angels weep, they rejoice when we die. I wrote this book after I'd asked God why there's not a day that I don't read about babies and people being raped, robbed or killed. I wrote this book because it's suppose to be a blessing to have a life. Busta Rhymes said "It ain't safe no more" and he's right. It ain't safe no more and we live in fear, we must take back our streets and protect our women, children and our homes and our communities. We must guide our children to the right paths in life. It's our duty and responsibility to make our neighborhoods safe. I remember back in the day we listened to the prophets and poets' words. There was magic in their words. Generations brought their children up by the word. Traditions were passed on and carried down, the words were the pillars of our lives and culture. Our culture was bathed in love, truth and respect. We honored our parents who worked hard to provide better lives for us, the coming generation. And now it ain't safe no more. Our babies stopped living by the word, they lost their trust, they stopped living their dreams. So I wrote this book shouting to the world, hoping my echo vibrates through the galaxies, hoping that you hear, hoping that you read, hoping that you feel the magic, the power of spoken words. I started writing poetry when I was about seven years old. I wrote to music like Little Richard and James Brown and any other good music. There was always a joy in painting, writing and early on it became my weapon of choice. If it wasn't for words and writing I would have been silent and invisible, nobody would have known I was there. So I took the words and I wrote about my friends and where I lived. I felt someone had to tell their story.

I wanted to give a purpose to their lives even if that purpose was to show the stupidity of their actions. I was a man-child when I saw the pimps and hustlers, I saw women working on the corners. My brother, 2row, would come home with money and tell me how he'd robbed somebody. We were poor, we were hungry but I wouldn't steal. I became a boxer, I was fast, I loved to dance around the ring and I read about all the great fighters, Archie Moore, Jack Johnson, Joe Louis, Sugar Ray Robinson. I trained in Mohammed Ali's gym and I wanted to be great like them but something was wrong, it wasn't the opponent, that was the easy part, depression and thoughts of death drove me away from boxing and I felt ashamed, like it was a waste of my life, but I went on writing, talking and fighting demons within me as we all have to do in this life. I wrote this book because there is a purpose in all of us. We all have a reason for being on earth. My purpose on earth is to write and paint and enjoy the company of good people. Peace and blessings to all of you. I hope you read my book and I hope it compels you to think and want a better life. About that question that I asked God, I'm still waiting for an answer.

ACKNOWLEDGMENTS

I'd like to thank God who is always with me and lives in my heart.

My mother (Ma'dea), Lillie-Mae, my father Jethro Morgan, my brothers Julius, Johnny, Larry, my sisters Mary and Janice and my son Jumaane.

My mom, Alegria Bendelac, who has helped me in many ways, her daughter Lisa who helped inspire this book and who has been there from start to finish. I'd like to thank Barry Huber for the wonderful photos and his wife Mercedes for her creative input.

Charles McGill, Wanda Scott Seay and her husband Nate Seay Jr., Valerie Brown O'Neal, James Cave (Caveman) and Bobby Robert, six wonderful friends who listened and encouraged me to go on further.

A special thanks to the Queens Community House Director, Dinah Morgan, and Bari Goltzman before her. The Queens Central Public Library, Inge Judd and Hugh Hamilton and WBAI Talkback radio in New York..

Poets & Writers for publishing my stories on line, their writing workshop, Bonnie Rose Marcus and Nancy Kline, the class leaders. The class Mildred Heller, Ruth Abrams, Joyce Burger, Bernice Blackwell, Dagmar Cermak, Enid Brownstone, Penny Cooper, Diana Graham, Phyllis Dennett, Mary Ann Plelan, Elaine Weintraub, Pearl Wolf, Phyllis Pumick for their encouragement, help, support and smiles.

A special thanks to Michael Alpiner and Eythan Klamka, fellow poets and teachers.John L. Todras a great pianist and Elizsabeth Ahne. Thelma Thomas and Dr. Joyce Duncan directors of the African Folk Heritage Circle. Thank you as well to Catherine Marks for her help and encouragement.

Herbert Hipp, a wonderful friend and nurse at the VA hospital, Barry Campbell who has generously helped me and thousands of veterans who needed his help.

I would also like to thank my nephews Tripp Morgan and Daniel Morgan, Jason Weaver, Jarrett Watkins, Vicky and Diana Gatson, Ed and Christopher Smith and everyone who graciously allowed me to use their pictures.

Thanks to all the people I've met along the way who smiled or frowned. Anyway it goes it's had a profound effect upon this book.

This book is dedicated to my mother Lillie-Mae (Ma'dea) and my mom Alegria Bendelac

WHAT IF I WAS A PROPHET

What if I was a prophet and I was taking the country by storm
What if the father's words were delivered in creative art form

The words are the food, the words are the dressing
I'm giving you his words with the father's blessing

I'm a prophet for the multitudes
Enjoy the words because the words are food

A prophet for you to hear
Hear me and your spirit will begin to heal
The power of words is what you will feel

HISTORY

NATIONS WILL RISE!

Nations will rise kingdoms will crumble
But if need be we'll build our kingdoms in the jungle.
Nations will rise kingdoms will crumble
One day the blessed earth shall belong to the humble

Tanzania Zaire farther north the Sudan
Once strong nations built by black men

Can a race be inferior with knowledge of Africa's interior?
Kenya was a Mecca of learning and education
Dry bones rise up you strong black nation

Go young seekers go and venture far
Explore exotic islands the land of Zanzibar
Search your mind search your soul
Feel the power unfold
Tell an ancient secret their stories must be told.

And you'll feel the utopia as you set foot in Ethiopia
With the glee of a child take a trip down the Nile
Africa our mother will make you smile
Now tear the myth asunder Uganda Rwanda
Africa our mother will be glad that you found her

Take a trip up the Congo the original Jurassic jungle
Enjoy the native sounds their dances and their bongos
But then with sadness you must go into the madness
Somalia will make you cry
As you witness the multitudes starve and die

Profits get promoted on babies' bellies bloated
Dying is a business that's marketed and sugar coated

Nations will rise kingdoms will crumble
But if need be we'll build our kingdoms in the jungle
Nations will rise kingdoms will crumble
One day the blessed earth shall belong to the humble

Nations will rise!

OH AFRICA

Oh Africa I cry under the bodies of black bodies

Your history lies

Oh Africa I am besieged by a mother's dire needs

Her children refugees a billion or more

Seeking aid from foreign shores

Oh Africa I cry as I watch a mother painfully die

Oh Africa I cry

RUNNING THROUGH THE BUSHES

Running through the bushes of the motherland
Africans being chased by Africans
I hear the pounding I feel the sweat, the sticky heat

The horrid screams the killing cry
Maybe it would have been better just to die

The cruel coarse cutting chain
Women and babies I feel their pain
The strong men weakened and whipped
Six hundred black slaves
On a trader's ship

Running through the bushes of the motherland
Africans being chased by Africans

BUFFALO SOLDIER

Buffalo soldier strong black boulder
Carried this country on your strong black shoulders
Buffalo soldier strong black boulder
Held this country when only we could hold her

More than ten thousand strong black men
Served in the ninth and the tenth cavalry
But this country never cared for me or my kind
You see justice was blind
Jim Crow rode with a closed mind
But seek and ye shall find
History of strong men like me in our chivalry
We were the twenty fourth and twenty fifth infantry

Listen to our spirits, listen too and you may hear it
The voice of Corporal Emanuel Stance
And the brothers whose lives he saved
From the lynch mob
We were lynched and we were robbed
Of our history which is a sin to me
So I cry when I see it
Brothers scared to be it soldiers boulders
And carry this country on your strong black shoulders

Buffalo soldier strong black boulder
Carried this country on your strong black shoulders
Buffalo soldier strong black boulder
Held this country when only we could hold her

WHEN LIONS ROAR

Look at our history look back and you'll adore
Look back upon times when lions roared.

Harriet Tubman, lion-hearted , she had to be
She lived in a world where you had to fight to be free
Frederick Douglas defiant of slavery to its core
I'm talking of times when lions roared

"Ain't I a woman" Sojourner Truth cried,
Yet they stole our manhood and shamed our pride
Covered us in scornful shame
Slavery you see could have no better name

The rich the poor stood in the way of freedom's door
With actions against us even they deplored
But I saw strong leaders
And again we heard the lions roar

I see our youth today many things I adore
But I wonder are there any lions anymore?
Are you afraid to roar?
Never forget your history knock down its very door
You are the lions and we need to hear you roar!

WE INTEGRATED SPORTS

We integrated sports and baseball
Pretty soon we thought that all America would be free
Treated equally but our timing was off
We couldn't integrate golf
Or their country clubs except to serve and scrub
Grin and please and satisfy their every need

Jim Crow was alive and swell living well
In suburbs
Negroes got what they deserved
Long years of jail and living hell

We jumped when the man rung the bell
We squeaked like mice when we stole a slice
Of American cheese
Even if it was diseased
Their nationality played on our mentality
Our fate and fatality our reality

We still sat at the back of the bus
In an unjust world we couldn't trust
On our own just us.
Stealing crumbs from the crust of American pie
Milk and honey for all when we die
That's the lie they told Negroes
In heaven who was gone milk the cows and gather the honey?

I'll bet you real money their Jesus would only need us
To keep his heaven in order and stay in the servants' quarters
Obey thy master for eternity pray for the guarantee
Quality of life free from America's strife

We integrated sports and baseball
But that was all freedom too has its cost

Mothers and babies suffered the loss
The absenteeism of fathers the slaughter
As our people wade in the water and call on Jesus
We say Father please don't leave us
In an unjust world we can't trust
On our own just us.
We integrated sports and baseball
But that was all

WE DANCED IN JUBILEE

We danced in jubilee whoopee for we were free

But black scent hung in southern breeze

Black bodies swung from southern trees

But Momma said there would be days like these.

So we kept moving pushing on

Kept on singing freedom's song

From lay-ins to pray-ins to picket lines

Today child it's your time to shine!

GRANDMA SAW VISIONS IN HER DREAMS

My great grandma saw visions in her dreams
She saw things of this world and things of other realms
She saw spiritual things she saw human beings
She saw her strong Negro nation
Suffering in segregation exploitation
My great grandma carried herself like a proud queen
But in her time cotton was king
Her husband was a loving Negro alcoholic
Who lived his life like the white man saw it
The way they called it
He worked the hot fields cotton and gin mills
From dark to dark his realities harsh
He got his gun when the hound dog barked
You see Jim Crow rode in the dark of night,
Hung any colored man he liked
Burned the house raped the lady
Shamed her with his near white baby
A bastard child no ifs or maybes
My great grandma saw visions in her dreams
One night she dreamt it she called it a white rock
She felt the panic the pain the pop
As her children's heartbeats were forced to stop
Their blood drip drop drain dry damn it die
She saw an angel cry
Shed its tears from the sky
For a billion souls that must need die
Though there be no reason why
She saw her babies cry in shame
In total ignorance of her name
Today sisters and brother man away from the motherland
Have forgotten all about their mothers mother man
But my great grandma saw visions in her dreams

From plantation to ghetto I hear slavery's echo
Henry Box Brown hiding in the shadow
And Redd Foxx spotted laughing in the meadow
B-I-G Lil' Kim Big Papa Proceed with Caution
Where once mothers grieved
Today we celebrate Foxy Brown Busta Rhymes and a cool Eve
Sister Sledge Jagged Edge We Pledge
Remember the love our fathers had
And wear his crown proudly upon our heads

From slave ships to showstoppers
Steppin' Fletcher Bojangles Big Papa
Muddy Waters James Brown lil' Bow Wow
We bow down bow down
For our heads still hold the Crown

Stand proud I heard him say

BARRY CAMPBELL

In 1860 a black slave hid in the late night shadows
Because he was brave
Klansmen rode in sheets of white
And they always came in the dark of night
They had come to hang this black slave high
And watch his body swing in the sky
This man whose mother named him Barry
And like all slaves had taught him to be wary
Of white men and their awful deeds.
White men loved to hear slaves plead,
But Barry insisted he was a man
Even if it meant being hung by the Klu Klux Klan
Barry's dreams and desires were the deliverance
Of slaves from slavery's fire

Today more than a century has passed
And I met a man named Barry Campbell
Who still refuses to wear the mask
Stand up he proclaimed to the veterans
You are men, that is your choice
I heard him speaking one day in his loud voice
"Help any man black or white
People in sheets still ride in the night
Help anyone for we are all brothers
This is the time to honor your father and mother"
"Stand proud" I heard him say
"It's a blessing to be born in this day"
He helped me as he helped all the others
He helped us as if we were brothers
And I will never forget that day
And that you heed his words is what I the poet pray

Quality of Life - Barry Campbell

LEST WE FORGET

Lest we forget in our ignorance submit
The long journey forces us to quit
Maybe upon a cozy fence we would rather sit
But remember the long march
Though the way was harsh
The lay-ins the pray-ins
The sub-human housing we were forced to stay in
The hell in jail a justice system failed
No vote no voice trapped no choice.
Our fear of dark nights
But there still was danger in the sunlight

Lest we forget compelled by our ignorance to sit out
But remember our fathers fought
With their backs against the wall
Fought hard for freedom for all
Freedom may it long live our voices risen high
In joyous union to the sky
Prejudice and bigotry forever lie
Limp lifeless dead
Along with the very ignorance that it bred
But of this foolishness I say simply enough said
Lest we forget.

IN YOUTH HE COULD DANCE

In youth he could dance and make the rhymes

He just couldn't whoop the passage of time

He floated like a butterfly, he stung like a bee

He was the greatest he was Muhammad Ali

I watched him fight throwing lightning lefts and rights

He brought something new to heavyweight fights

He was so fast and he talked so much

And we loved him because he was one of us

In youth he could dance and make the rhymes

He just couldn't whoop the passage of time

MANCHILD IN THE PROMISED LAND

I was a man child in the promised land
My momma scrubbed on knees and hands
For a dollar, she got a few every hour
But when momma got her money
Momma didn't have no power
She dreamt of islands being serenaded by violins
Lobster dinners vacation every winter
But life was rough we grew up we had enough
We gave up we turned corrupt
What's up what's up?
We were broke stand in line
Broke standing waiting where demons find
Idle minds festered on petty crime
You say so you do time don't whine
Just feel the pain of the mothers crying
And the fate of brothers dying
You blew that G away that day hey you don't play
What more need a brother say
I feel no power as I send flowers
But flowers should grow to light
Not cover graves in the night
And you fight your plight in a single cell
Where you your soul and demons dwell

Bloody visions predicated by conditions of sad traditions
Of just yourself and no one else
For goodness' sake we hate a jerk who puts in works
That hurts our lives, destroy husband family wives
Disrupt order as people scramble for quarter rocks to block
Ease the shock of what's not reality
You and me who can't be our all

Now let me tell you the truth about my youth
I was a man child in the promised land
Momma scrubbed on knees and hands
For a dollar she got a few every hour
But when momma got her money
Momma didn't have no power

MOMMA WAS A STRONG TREE

Momma was a strong tree strong tree
The best part of me for the world to see
Momma was a strong tree, strong tree
She was good wood, all good
Raised her kids the best she could
Good wood of a strong tree, strong tree
And that would be you and me

Thinking about my momma Urseline Adams
The deep down darkness of her pains I can't fathom
Alberta Hunter Tina Turner I still see Sojourner Truth
Proof that today our youth mustn't forget the very root
Key to the root of the fruit of a strong tree, strong tree
And that would be you and me

Mary McLeod Bethune Septima Clark
Thank you for lighting the torch in the dark
Shirley Graham DeBois stood up and made some noise
Michelle Obama our African American First Lady
We've come a long way no ifs or maybes
Bessie Smith started a new blues reaction
I heard it in the voice of Mahelia Jackson
Toni Braxton and B.B. King's Lucille
I saw it in the face of Camille Cosby
So it must be trust me
More than just me who can see
What once was and what it could be
Condeleeza Rice and Lena Horne
And everyday another nubian star is born
Do you remember the way things was
Never forget Dr. Betty Shabazz nor the journey we took
Through a poetry book
Discovering the joys the love of Gwendolyn Brooks
Hey sister I'm with you Maya Angelou

I wouldn't take nothing for my journey now too
Butterfly McQueen (String Bean) Ethel Waters
Our mothers got more respect on European borders
And the hoo-doo the voodoo that you do
Lauryn Hill and Erica Badu like Fu-bu
Our mothers stood by you
So no matter what you do
Don't wait show the Universe a fruit
From a tree that's great
Thinking about my momma the other day
The deep down darkness of her pains our mothers had to pay
I was thinking about my mother Lillie-Mae

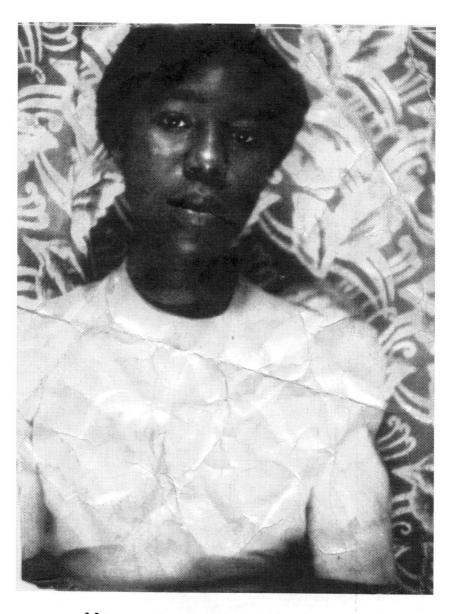

My momma was a strong tree strong tree
The best part of me for the world to see
Lillie-Mae (Ma'dea), my mother

IN THE SIXTIES

In the sixties we wore bell bottoms we were the flower child
Running wild Jimi Hendrix Purple Haze in useless ways
In the sixties we were the Motown sound,
We were Curtis Mayfield moving on up
Marching to a new vibrations across a racist nation
Looking at ourselves for salvation

In the sixties we were merging we were clever
Damn it if the system didn't murder Medgar Evers
And Martin went to the mountain but couldn't get to the top
But instilled dreams never to stop
Climbing high into the sky
Keep on climbing until the day you die!

In the sixties we were Nikki Giovanni Harry Belafonte
The natural cultural Afros no more neutral Negroes
Aretha said it "All we wanted was a little respect"
R-E-S-P-E-C-T damn what that couldn't do for me
A little T-L-C makes you want to T-C-B
Because nothing's stronger than L-O-V-E

In the sixties we broke the laws we changed the text
We were Adam Clayton Powell
The Southern Christian Leadership Conference
We were CORE we were the poor
At the rich man's door
We were Langston Hughes "Dream Deferred"
To some we were simply Negroes with a lot of nerves

In the sixties we were the cry in the dark
We marched for our mothers and Rosa Parks
We were Dick Gregory H. Rap Brown
In the sixties we were the new sheriff in town
We were the unborn babies in the womb
The African slaves in the tomb
The couldn't find work fathers who couldn't stay
Like sweet nights' dreams gone away

In the sixties it was a new day for religion
As a new sunlight glistened
And we turned to the East
With Elijah Muhammad's nation of Islam
We were Eldridge Cleaver's "Soul on Ice"
Defying America for a slice of the pie
But we wanted it now before we die
In the sixties black power was the word
Most often heard as we burned city streets
Angry at a society that wouldn't allow us fairly to compete
In markets of merger as merchants bought
Traded and made their sales
Angry at a society that saw us only as heathens
More suited for jails

In the sixties...

A STRANGE LAND

I am my ancestors' eyes

I am their prize

I am the dream realized

I still hear the echo sounding

The deep base drum pounding

Never forsaken

A hollow place in my soul awakened

Five hundred years and finally a man

Lord Lord Lord what a strange strange land.

AND THE BEAT DON'T STOP

And the beat don't stop we keep climbing to the top
Of corporate ladders turning cheese into cheddar
Our pocket getting fatter birth of a nation a celebration
I'm speaking to a Barack nation I'm talking to a new generation

So prepare for the race I'm speaking of your dreams
And of the dreams you chase
It's your life take a taste be a part of the race
And the beat don't stop

But up and down the avenues
Folks having trouble with revenues
Folks singing the blues
They don't know what they gone do
Their babies in school because education rules

And the beat don't stop so drop your gun son
Prison life ain't no fun ain't no life on the run
Commit a crime and your life is done
You'll march to the beat
In a cell or on the streets
And the beat don't stop

We keep climbing and climbing
Climbing to the top
And the beat don't stop

It's the B to the bop it's the hip to the hop
An Obama generation climbing to the top
And the beat don't stop

And the Beat Don't Stop

INNER CITY

A CHILD'S DREAM

With a switch a blade a machete
I dreamt I hunted with lions on the Serengeti
In the highland I camped with gorillas
I never heard words in reference to niggas
Our universal God is good our mother delivers
As a child I remember cut throats thugs and killers
Drug wars drug lords and drug dealers

Momma smoked a rock but the stuff wouldn't heal her
In about a year that shit gone kill her
A black box is where we'll seal her
In a black car is how we'll wheel her
And Father Time passing will seem like a blessing
As we learn to forgive her
Forgive but not forget that harsh hateful shit
If only momma would have quit
Lord knows they took her quick

Now with a grain of sand of stone my pyramid rise
I submit as one to the all seeing eye
Healer of heaven earth skies I rise
For how could I die?
And with a spic a speck of my sweat
I sat and watched it form the Nile
It ran down my black body as a child as I smiled
Onward on its quest downward down my chest
Past eagles' nest
As I sat bedazzled it finally settled
Where I lived
Brown broke boy with nothing to give
Livid life lived for taking prison life in the making
Black boy minority torn from the majority
No job seniority ancestors royalty
Who instilled loyalty while creatively creating creativity

Joyous festivity amidst hostility
Loved all equally
In the land of the brave home of the free
But it didn't include me

But I was a child and so I smiled
And dreamt of swimming with crocodiles in the Nile

I WENT TO MY BROTHER

I went to my brother to ask for help
The help that he gave was I better help myself
Now I write lyric like musical notes
Hear the words to my thoughts and what they promote
My words make people sit up
I write about life and inner city get up

Justice is never demanding
It's a rough feeling of rhythm and understanding
Today my brothers doing the same old same old
Getting over down in the ghetto
Still making signs of a loser
Told me the other day that he was a Hoover Crip
Like it was hip
Selling drugs to our nation spiritual masturbation
A quick and easy ejaculation of our manhood
It feels good but it produces nothing
There I think I hit it right on the button

Billions abandoned babies buried
The damnation of addiction is scary
Intravenous feeding fetus drugs
Babies born in worlds with no love
Worlds of conflict and pain
I think their souls just want to leave this plane
Than to remain prisoners to parents with nothing to give
The soul needs love to thrive and live

Locked up locked in locked out
A child remembers what it's been taught
Never learning to read
Nah that's not what a lost soul need
He's dreaming an Uzi in his Jacuzzi
A sawed- off and telling folks where to get off

Wit, grit and bullshit, simple mind give in and quit
But the strong never submit
Turn up your nose turn down your thumb
Forget about where you come from
You don't hear the mothers crying
Fuck the fool hearted dying
Life's a fine wine to sip
It's OK to be hip
My brothers are dying so here's my tip
Protect our homes protect our streets
Men and women take a stand
Our children are being killed all over this land
I went to my brother to ask for help
The help that he gave was I better help myself

DAMN I BEEN SHOT!

Damn I been shot but I always knew the streets were hot
This ain't no game bullets don't have names.
The chances of my survival were slim upon my arrival
Into this world be I a boy or girl
Life has few prospects when it's started in a project
And so you say we're having fun
But don't you know a poor man's grief weighs tons
On minds in a blind world where unkind boys and girls
Pearls, children of the world
Are willing to continue the killing
.

Damn I been shot my momma to watch me die
Forever to ponder the question why
Her heart and soul to wrench and cry
Demons wrestle with her soul alone now no son to hold
A mother's voice with no recourse
But to call Jabreel Jabreel where did he go?
We love you so

Damn I been shot at the wrong place at the wrong time
The city's news filled with news of dying
Today KKK means kids killing kids
Cool colored kids
They'll never know the harm they did
The descendants of slaves killing descendants of slaves
But to survive we must be brave
One by one fight to save just one life
Destroy the gun take away the knife
End the strife preserve our lives
Wipe away the tears end the fears
And baby maybe in the years to come
To be proud where we come from
Damn I been shot, kids killing kids killing kids killing kids
Damn I been shot!

GENIE MAC GENIE MAC

It started before elementary
Genie Mac headed for the penitentiary
Still in the infant stage at an early age
He felt the burning rage of a wounded beast
That stalks between the cage

He was forced through the tunnels of life
So he figured it best to cop a piece a shank a knife
Genie Mac out on the tracks
Once you're turned out you can't turn back
Genie Mac out on the tracks
And every brother you know got a monkey on his back
Genie Mac Genie Mac Genie Mac

When he was thirteen he was five foot seven
He started out robbing a 7 Eleven
Nervous with a rusty gun
But a man child gotta do what's gotta be done

His brother told him never to cry
He said don't ask no questions why
He said first we live and then we die
Said the weak get pushed along
Jailed in their barred up homes
Crying about societal wrongs
He said " my brother" He said "Be strong"

Genie Mac out on the block
Selling the rocks a quarter a pop
Dressed down in his jock his stash in his sock
Business done with a glock
And if your fool ass gets popped
Well Genie's cash flow won't stop
I look back it makes no sense to me
Genie Mac headed for the penitentiary
Genie Mac Genie Mac Genie Mac

MAD RUSH

I remember the mad rush my boy Chris got caught flush
In the chest and just like that a mere minute of a sec.
A split second of a flash before you could bat an eye
Or hear a mother's cry I saw my boy Chris die

I saw the priest read him his last rites
Right there on the scene of the death site
If he could have just held tight maybe in the night fight
Instead I saw his soul walk into the light

And just like that a mere minute of a sec.
A split second of a flash before you could bat an eye
Or hear a mother's cry I saw my boy Chris die

We always wanted to be drug kings
We said God made rocks for us to sling
We were men at sixteen
We had a whole lot of queens
We were the cream of the crop
We said even the law couldn't make us stop
Then that night my boy got popped

And just like that a mere minute of a sec.
A split second of a flash, before you could bat an eye
Or hear a mother's cry I saw my boy Chris die

I remember the mad rush my boy Chris got cold crushed
He turned to me as if to touch
Those final seconds meant so much
I saw his soul but you don't believe in such

And just like that a mere minute of a sec.
A split second of a flash before you could bat an eye
Or hear a mother's cry I saw my boy Chris die

"Before you could bat an eye or hear a mother's cry I saw my boy Chris die"

LOVE, YOUR SON CHRIS

Dear Momma,

I'm sorry I just couldn't do right
My life it seems was just one long fight
Things I couldn't do
Things I just couldn't see
I guess momma it was hard being me.

I remember you said I wouldn't live to be twenty
Well you were right momma
So just bury me with a box of Good & Plenty
A love letter from my lady
A picture of my baby
I'm going to miss her momma, no ifs or maybes
But I'll be there momma to watch her grow
I'll be there she just won't know

And momma I'll miss you too
All the wonderful things I saw you do
A prayer over every meal
I love you momma but this gunshot wound won't heal

Tell Tanya I wish she was my wife
Tell her to go on and find a good man and live a good life
Momma I'm your angel to watch over you in the sky
Momma I'm sorry I had to die

                    Love, your son
                    Chris

ANOTHER BROTHER GOT SHOT

Another brother got shot last night
He didn't run but he didn't fight
He gave up the goods
The thugs knew that he would
You see thugs rule the neighborhood.

Another brother got shot last night
It happened so fast that as he took his last breath
He felt the cold hand of slow death
Neither cold nor hot as paralysis hit the spot
And so he stopped he dropped, out on the city streets
Chilled in the city's heat looking up at people's feet

Knowing he was dying and so he just stopped trying
He heard voices faded his vision jaded,
A few more blocks and he would have made it
He felt so weak he couldn't feel his feet
He uttered sounds but he couldn't speak

Another brother got shot last night
He didn't run but he didn't fight
The thugs took what he had
And then they shot him dead
They fled into the night
Feeling power of ungodly might
Laughing when they should have been crying
This is the season of untimely dying
Laughing as we the living mourn
As families find ways to carry on
The morning paper read city youth shot dead
Thugs took what he had, they fled into the night
Feeling power of ungodly might
Another brother got shot last night

DOWN IN THE GHETTO

Down in the ghetto they say we don't care
They say hey colored kids don't comb their hair
They tell their kids "Don't you go down there"
They got pushers they got punks out on the streets
They got crooked cops that be patrolling the beat

Con men hustlers trying to make a score
Peacock preachers out robbing the poor
You better watch out they'll take what's yours
Down in the ghetto

Down in the ghetto where I was born
Always something going on
A big time thug robbed a bank
I helped an old lady she didn't even say thanks
They beat an old man with a metal pole
They busted him in the head because he was old
Now everyone's scared to come out the house
You're the cat and we're the mouse
But you say if things get better you'll make it so
Then you'll tell us where we can go

Go to church on Sunday work on Monday
Party on the weekend forget about sin
Then come Monday you start all over
And you do it all again
Down in the ghetto

Down in the ghetto where I was raised
Folks walking around in a daze
And in the summer I can't take the smell
Thank goodness for color or I would be pale
Why be concerned about a bigger jail
When you've got us living in your hell
Down in the ghetto.

ON THE DIRTY SIDEWALK

On the dirty sidewalk was a stain

The dried up blood of her brain

Twelve years lived and killed

The preacher said it was as God had willed

He said God's will would always be done

But would God will kids killed by guns

Along came a torrential rain but it couldn't wash away the stain

Nor the remains the dried up blood of her brain

A simple reminder life could be a lot kinder

A mother searching for her child

But nowhere can she find her

Along came a torrential rain but it couldn't wash away the stain

Nor the remains the dried up blood of her brain

IN THE WINTER

In the winter the snow gets high
And more of that stuff keeps falling from the sky
The roaches and rats got fur coats too
And if you're meek and humble
They'll take yours from you

Three winos on the corner froze to death
One bottle of wine couldn't warm themselves
I needed money for my rent but it all got spent
And I'm still wondering where it all went
Electric and gas shot sky high
Folks don't care if I live or I die
My kids all hungry I know I gotta cheat
Everybody knows kids gotta' eat

The first of the month there's A.D.C.
They act like they're giving the world to me
Medicare Medicaid the folks downtown
Think I got life made
I went downtown to get my food stamps
Everyone there got treated like tramps
A stuck-up broad said what I was good for
And that's when I realized " This is war!"

I want to be decent but I can't find a job
The only way to live is steal and rob
Times are hard times are lean
Good home folk turning mean
Bars on the windows cameras on the doors
Even in the cold you gotta' protect what's yours

Mean watchdog lurking in the yard
But his ass in danger because times are hard
I went outside to get something to eat
And when I got back home they cut off the heat
Later that night off goes the gas
And now I know it's over for my black ass

I hurry to the bathroom in a great big rush
And then the damn toilet won't even flush
Everything's out of order the stove don't work
Can't even boil water

And more of that stuff keeps falling from the sky

Folks in the family say I'm not kin
And to blame myself for the fix I'm in
They say find some work you stupid jerk
They say read the paper they say stay alert
They say take any job don't worry about the pay
And bye and bye things will be OK

I went on a job an interview and they outright told me
"We don't hire folk like you"
To make a long story short I'll have to go to court
And the judge looks down on things of this sort
I'm out on the street I'm trying to hustle up the bread
There's a lot of sick things going through my head

The snow's still falling
Seems like I hear my babies calling
I better keep moving and quit this stalling
It's so cold not a cop on patrol,
Not even a whore working the stroll

The whole damn city's all snowed under
Can I survive 'til spring hey I wonder

I walk and I walk until I'm frozen stiff
Will I get the money? That's a great big if
Brother on the corner got a dime bag to sell
I just tell him to go to hell

Finally after walking all day
I spot me an easy prey an old lady with a cane
I don't want to do it but I've got hunger pains
I thought about my momma my sisters too
I wouldn't like it if it were mine hey would you?

I thought about my friends and the fixes they were in
Conway's dead got shot in the head
And Johnny's still serving time
Doing free labor until he changes his behavior
And like all poor folk he's still waiting for a savior
Now the man want to lock me up
Because society says I'm corrupt
Lock me away as long as it can
I guess my kids don't need a daddy?
The state won't release me until it's ready

And my woman don't need a man
She can find her loving where she can
But kids seem to grow up wrong
When there's no fathers in the home
In the winter the snow gets high
And more of that stuff keeps falling from the sky

TELL ME WHY TELL ME WHY

The bullet smashed through my skull
I felt the burning blast of the slug
Fire burning in my brain instant panic sudden pain
But in the morning only a body would remain

I know I'm gone die gone meet my maker in the sky
Gone get my piece of the pie will my soul rise on high?
Or is it done when we die?
I'll never open up my eyes
Or see my babies baptized I hope you realize
That they are punished and chastised

Tell me why tell me why
Another brother gotta die gotta die
Tell me why tell me why
Another brother gotta die

Yesterday a baby got shot
Thirteen people killed on the same block
And every year as long as I remember
More death in the summer and the middle of December
Now when I hear the booming hi-fi no lie I cry
I wonder why I got to die in a drive-by

But here I am and here I lie
The sad thought the sad refrain
A burning bullet in the brain
But in the morning only a body would remain
Now tell me why tell me why?

TWO DOPE DEALERS DEAD

It was a dope deal gone bad

And now two dope dealers dead

Four ounces of lead

Blood gushing from the head

We ought to be mad

Understand the pain as they bled

Understand what led

To the event it wasn't no accident

Just two dealers dead

The paper said the suspect fled

But it feels like treason for no reason it's hunting season

On black men

We're like Christians in the lion's den

But we ought to know better

We can't all climb corporate ladders

We can't all play basketball

Dance or sing

Do you know what I mean?

It was just a dope deal gone bad

My two brothers shot in the head

But it was just a dope deal gone bad

A SILLY RHYMING POEM

There's no hair on my head
My room is painted red
But what more need be said
I call my uncle Jed
He has a brother whose name is Ned

My fish in the aquarium are kept fed
I took a shower under my new showerhead
I stubbed my toe and it bled

I could kill my cousin but he fled
I searched for him out by the shed
I saw my horse whose name is Ed
And then I saw my uncle Jed
He was with his brother whose name is Ned

Then I saw my brother Fred
Who once had an arrow stuck in his head
Boy! That had to hurt that's what I said
My sister Meg got the news and she was glad
When she's happy I get scared
Her happiness is what I dread

I thought that was why my cousin fled
As I told his father Jed
Who told it to his brother whose name is Ned
Then they went to pick up Fred
He's the one who had the arrow stuck in his head
He looked at me and he looked mad
So I said hey brother Fred,
What's up uncle Jed? Hey uncle Ned
And they all laughed at my bald head
There's no hair on my head
Because cousin Craig cut it before he fled.

CONWAY

Conway couldn't write the brother couldn't read

Book learning understand ain't what a brother need

He needs a knife a piece a gun

Survival is real and it ain't fun

Pack that steel heavy and long

You got to be right you can't afford to be wrong

Go down and rob the liquor store

You make the man behind the counter

Get down on the floor

Then you take your girl to dinner

It feels good to be a winner

But maybe tomorrow you'll go to jail

And serve the devil in a living hell

Or maybe tomorrow you'll come up dead

One well placed bullet in the head

The jails are filled the graves are too

With closed minded brothers just like you

A RIOT

I sat in deathly silence

The cruel world around me filled with violence

I heard the rapid pops of gunshots

Everything around me stopped

They killed another young boy

And all around me was war

What could I a helpless child do?

So I sat angry thinking in deathly silence

But inside of me there was a riot

I'M AN ORPHAN

I'm an orphan but my parents aren't dead

Years ago my father fled

And the death of my mother

Were the mean words that she said

FATHER WAS A GOOD MAN

My father Jethro was a good man,
He always did the best he could
But no matter how hard the times
My father always found something good
To say to talk about
There's this silly rumor when I was a child,
That my father just walked out
But my father found a world cruel unyielding
My father found that white society found
His black skin so unappealing

So my Father found back alley crap games
Late night liquor loose women willing
Money that came fast but went quicker
When I was a boy my momma used to say
"Boy you're just like your no-good daddy"
He never had a job or earned a living steady
But to me my father could do anything, fix anything
There was nothing he couldn't do
He was my black God but my father was a man I never knew

I used to watch all the women with all the different men
I heard the sounds of their happiness and the joys of their sins
Morning came and the men were gone
And struggling single black women had better get on
Today I too am a man caught up in the struggle
With so many lives and loose ends to juggle
My father once tall and proud bent by heavy years' worry
A shorty long in his back pocket
If you don't understand it it's cool just don't knock it
Today my father bowed head eyes red,
The look of the living dead
I feel the pain of what my father once had and lost
The exacting cost of his own father's sin

Which today as far as I can see are visited upon me

Yeah my father was a good man always did the best he could
But in a world wherein he had no voice
My father was deeply misunderstood
Forced to stay in places society felt he should stay
And thus today I find a society still that way
My father Jethro was a good man

THICK LIP WEATHERED AND TORN

Thick lip red and orange

Weathered skin beaten and torn

Eyes that's done seen all there is to see

When I look at you brother I see me

Ain't nothing worse than a man forget who he is

Then pass his sins on down to his kids

Hair ain't never seen a comb

If I got a new suit I got it on loan

Look in the mirror brother what do you see

I know I know you see me

STILL WAITING FOR A CHANGE MAN

Father was a voodoo man
A thick-lipped Cajun man
A healing magical hands man
A spiritual dancing man
A chased and jailed man
All over this land man

Father was a troubled mystery man
Always on his knees and hands man
He was a Lord if only I can man
Father was a pleading man
A sore hearted bleeding man

A Negro man some say evil man
He was a before his times man
Now he's an old deranged man
But he's still waiting for a change man

WHEN YOU'RE DOWN AND OUT

When you're down and out
There's something you should know
I know a place you can always go
There's never too much for you to bear
You see your heavenly father he's always there
So just remember when the spirit seize us
To call on him in the name of Jesus.

He's someone that you can trust
Just call his name say Jesus Jesus
Life isn't always kind sometimes justice is blind
Young blood about to go out of your mind
You're looking all over for some kind of sign
But you see the punks and the pushers out on the street
Everybody it seems is under some kind of heat
Dope man on the corner looking for his flunkies
Brother aren't you glad you're not a junky

There's never too much for you to bear
You see your heavenly father he's always there
So just remember when the spirit seizes us
To call on him in the name of Jesus
He's someone that you can trust
Just call his name say Jesus Jesus

MOMMA DANCED

Momma danced a slow voodoo ritual
In a modern world of computers and digitals
Did you know her father's father listened over radio
Drank his old crow
Prayed to a blue-eyed God he did not know
Prayed that white folks would let go
Of their racist Jim Crow
And then well who knows
What a man who lived off the land
Worked with his hands
Took care of his clan could command

Momma's mother sang an old gospel hymn
She sang though the living was dim the pickings slim
She prayed that one son would be able
To bring food to his table
Look a white man in the eye
And in the night not have to die
Momma danced a slow voodoo ritual
In a modern world of computers and digitals

My grandma prayed that white folks would let go of their racist Jim Crow

My grandmother Katie Mae Miller

I'M SCRAMBLING

I'm scrambling I'm on a mission on a run
I'm gambling my addiction's a loaded gun
People fear me won't come near me
The law won't clear me
Scared I might just do them harm
You may have read last night
Another junkie mother bought the farm
Eyes red kind of sad always happy never glad
I won't stop til I drop gotta cop gone pop
If I'm lucky I'll feel the shot hot hit the spot
Forever stop another junkie mother from the block

I'm scrambling I'm on a mission on a run
I'm gambling my addiction's a loaded gun
Hey you don't know what I know
You can't go where I go
But you know I go where the dope flows
And the 5-0 the po-po they know
So we keep it on the down low
I share no shame I take no blame
This ain't no game fuck my name
You don't know my pain
Nor the womb of whence I came

I have no charm I mean no harm
You may have read last night
Another junkie mother bought the farm
I'm scrambling I'm on a mission on a run
I'm gambling my addiction's a loaded gun

OUR LIVES WERE SO SWEET

Our lives were so sweet we thought that they were never ending
But what we took for granted was only the beginning
Of lives of crime and brothers OD'ing and dying
When we were younger we used to kick it
Old folks today just won't admit it
They got those phony self-righteous acts and they need to quit it
We enjoyed the fruit of the wine of our time
Now we're living in another generation
And we're weak and we're dying

Some of us went down with the sawed-off stick-up
Some of us were so weak we just couldn't get up
Some of us were nothing more than the man wrote on paper
Politicians say lockup all the inner city youths
And make our city streets safer
I used to fantasize of super heroes and capes
But the concrete jungles offered little escape
My momma my sisters' lives are in danger
They could be molested or killed by a total stranger

Little girls little boys coming up missing
We're being killed everyday
But folks won't listen
They found a lady her body cut up in pieces
I felt the family pain I got a mother sisters and nieces
I sit and I wonder as the days pass
Every moment could be my last

There's a message and it needs to be heard
Because back in the day
We lived by the word
Our lives were so sweet we thought that they were never ending

I LOOK AROUND ME

I look around me I see the faces of my ancestors
Like I'm holding court sequestered
Thrust back into the yesterdays
Repeating the penalty and the phase
Color folk ignorant of white ways
I wonder and I vent but it doesn't put a dent
In the minds of fools content
Sometimes I wonder where the good old days went

When we marched we fought we died
But we did so with pride
Even just a lay-in if nothing more than a pray-in
Their bombs, their clubs, couldn't hold us back
You see it was the injustice that we attacked
Determined as a race to get up off our backs our knees
Put an end to the disease of neutral Negroes only bound to please
We stretched we shuffled and we gestured
Our women worked because the system let them
Wash, iron and scrub on knees bent over a washtub
But oh the Master we loved

I look around me I see the faces of my ancestors
Like I'm holding court sequestered
But this is a new day and a new date
Jim Crow has died but we're still fighting his hate
I look around me I see the faces of my ancestors

BUSTED

Busted but I knew I couldn't find me no justice

Busted bound over and accosted

I'm jailed until the keys are rusted

In jail and I'm pissed got me a hit list

Who knows maybe I'll slit my wrist

Folks call me snake 'cause I hiss

I never enjoyed a woman and her sweet kiss

In jail and ain't no bail

I'll never leave this cell

Folks pray that my soul rot in hell

Busted but I knew I couldn't find me no justice

Bound over and accosted

Jailed until the keys are rusted

Son this is worse than hell

Ain't no life in a prison cell

This ain't college

Don't come here looking for some knowledge

Here you might be somebody's wife

If that's what you want then enjoy your caged up life

Busted but I knew I couldn't find me no justice

BLACK COMEDIANS

From sun up to sun down their sweat watered the ground
We smiled no frowns our sweat built this town
Our love was bittersweet we laughed with
Mom's Mabley and Pigmeat
Like a phoenix we rise in love and no reprise
Slappy White Dolemite we laugh
Thankful for what we have

Nipsey Cosby Eddy our George Wallace
We walk we will our kids to college
Seeking knowledge and a bit of polish
When they're up there's no drainer
Boy we laughed with Cedric the Entertainer

Steve Harvey took the sadness out of me
And Bernie Mac if only we could bring him back
From sun up to sundown you people stole the town
With Laughter and relief
You wonderful people are thieves

Chris Tucker brother he made you laugh sucker
The Wynan brothers and super soul sister Mo'nique
Whoopi DL Hughley and Martin Lawrence
Which do I need more I wonder laughter or life insurance?
And Kat Williams we miss you
We're still laughen'
You're a part of the fun we're having
You stole our hearts you warmed our souls
You people are worth more than your weight in gold.

You stole our hearts you warmed our souls

SPIRITUAL

IT'S TIME FOR ALL MEN

Wake up wake up wake up in a black night

Bathe your soul in the white light

Let your soul take flight

To new heights and new horizons

Heavenly father hear the prayers I send

It's time for all men to transcend back into being Gods again

Forgive us for our sins, color of our skin

With the passion of love all hurts and hearts can mend

If we believe in love then we can cleanse

Mankind and dirty minds

You say you love but still you're blind

This is the day this is the time

Our mothers prayed for our fathers paid for

Now all can walk through the same door

Into the light let your soul take flight

To new heights and new horizons

Heavenly father hear the prayers I send

It's time for all men to transcend back into being Gods again

MY SOUL IS A GIANT

My soul is a giant it needs to be heard
Nothing has more power than the spoken word
My soul is crying can not you hear
Have the sounds of my thoughts muffled your ears
Inside my soul is in a rage
I pray you be wise and not open my cage

My soul is angry at God's betrayal
I bear this cross for a soul that's frail
My soul is a predator it pounces it fights
My soul needs resting on a sleepless night

My soul is a giant it needs to be heard
Nothing has more power than the spoken word

WE SING

We sing when our voices no longer can be heard
We sing because in the beginning there was the word
We sing when our voices are coarse and dry
We sing sometimes when even we don't know why we sing
Sing sing a sad song
Sing it gladly until the pain is gone

Tell God of our frustrations
Sing a song of souls' salvation
Sing in hunger and our belly aches
Sing if the earth trembles and quakes
Sing sing in your sleep
Sing if your precious soul the Lord don't keep

We sing when our voices no longer can be heard
We sing because in the beginning there was the word
So we sing

GOD'S CHILD

We are all God's child

God's smile

God's children of the Nile

Our fathers of Zion

Hunted with lions

We are God's smile

God's child

God's children of the Nile.

God's children of the Nile

THE WOMAN

When God made man, the man found that he was lonely
And the grandest of Gardens wasn't a happy home
So God spoke the man into a peaceful sleep
And promised him his soul to keep
From the man God took a rib
For God's last creation, the woman
The man too had to give
You see the woman was an omen
A precious gift created within a sacred precious moment
And God was praised
And the man too knew he was blessed
To live out his days
With God's most precious gift
The woman

LET HER GET CLOSE

Let her get close as close as a breeze touch to soft skin caress
As close as universes and time forever moving and forever one

Within self wanting calling whatever love needs to grow
Within the confines of a soul's journey to you
Let her get close

Let her get close as close as planets full joyous triumphant
In the wetness of beaches' warm shores
Her horizons cool, calm, calling
Let her get close

Let her get close as close as the sea is to the sand
And winds to carry her name upon its breezes
Let her feel the drums of Africa's soul vibration

Dancing beating in universal darkness rhythm
Knowing tomorrow's sunrise will brighten minds' eyes
Heat passions yearning fruit sweet needs
Let her get close
Let her get close as close as love is to the heart
A child's dream sweetheart sweet tarts
Smell love's fire pure hot wild retained
Caught up in a soul's refrain
For who tell me who would know love's name.
Let her get close

And the man too knew that he was blessed

I FEEL SPIRITS

I feel spirits as I pray I thank you lord for this blessed day
Thank you for the soul of Joseph Cinque
Kunta Kinte Denmark Vesey Nat Turner
Harriet Tubman our Moses she told us
God chose us in a world where only God knows us
Paul Robeson, Dorothy Dandridge
I feel the way you once did
A black man had to cross the ocean
To cross the racial bridge

Bessie Coleman "Queen's Bee"
Ulysses Kay Isaac Hayes Willie Mays
Ida Bell Wells William Grant Still
Anita Hill, Emmet Till Peace be still

Lift every voice and sing
Praise the soul of Martin Luther King
Benjamin Banneker Marian Anderson
Claude McKay Lady Day Sugar Ray
Duke and Ella Sarah Vaughan
And our joys go on and on

He floated like a butterfly he stung like a bee
Child your hands can't hit what your eyes can't see
I'm speaking of 'the greatest' Mohammad Ali

Elijah the real McCoy and here's to your mama's baby boys
Marcus Medgar Miles Malcolm and Malcolm's daughters
Hold on child you got to wade in the water

Lorraine Hansberry Matthew Henson Althea Gibson,
Jackie Wilson Marvin Gaye we miss you man today
Jack Johnson Joe Louis your spirit flows through us
You would feel it too if only you knew us
To Satchel and Satchmo and all buffalo soldiers I know
Zora Neale Hurston and to all mothers' sons whose eyes have seen
Pain as well as joyous things past and present Kings and Queens
Run DMC Ice Cube Ice Tea
The Notorious B-I-G Easy-E Master P Heavy D Jay Z
P Diddy Snoop Dogg 2 Pac
We cried when the music stopped
It's our soul Queen Latifah's flavor we can't stop creative behaviors
It's our blues, our jazz, Josephine Baker's pizzazz
Louis and Carl Stokes in our grief we joked
Richard Pryor lived the words his soul spoke
And Noble Drew Ali and you and me

One hundred million souls lost in the slave trade
Never forget those dreadful days
We descendants of Kings and Queens
Considered cattle half human being
In a land of no justice
Thank God for W.E.B., Booker T and Douglass
For God saw that it was all good

Thurgood Marshall and Carter G. Woodson
Wanted the world to know
That we as a nation would only grow
I feel spirits as I pray.
I thank you Lord for Beyonce Kid 'n Play
Doctor J. Macy Gray
And my mother Lillie-Mae
I feel spirits as I pray

Though I may stumble
Though I may fall

GLORY LIGHT

Glory light gospel light

Lead me Lord through the night

Though the pathway is darkened

The enemy hearken

What benefits a man whose gains are ill gotten

Though I may stumble

Though I may fall

I will rise Lord when you call

Glory light gospel light

Lead me Lord through the night

LIFE OF THE SOUL

On this earth we all face the same thing

The same shame the same pain

On this earth we age and we change

We come onto the earth filled with life

And then we are slowly drained

I asked God because I wanted to know why

I heard him say

Son That's the only way I could compel a soul

To want to go on throughout the galaxies

Your soul will discover in wonder my endless creations

So go on son and enjoy this life

WE SHINE

I see you brothers with your so call cool cold walk
Like whatever it be about it don't be about your fault
Standing demanding, on the corners the bus stops,
Listening to bee bop hip hop nonstop
Rhyming words splitting verbs have you heard
What disturbs our minds
Mankind in our time seeking still peace sublime
Though still though we shine

I see you brothers with your cell phones but none at home
Listening to Biggie and Bones
Braids crowning your dome
Your laughter don't hide your moan
One lost lone soul cold old before its time
Caught up in lyric of rhythm and rhyme
While seeking still peace sublime
Though still though we shine

I see you brothers at the funeral parlors
You make me want to holler throw up both my hands
Don't you understand our misgiving your degraded living?
Mr. O.G. gangster ignorant prankster silly lyrics fill your head
You glad another brother dead
He was too young to go that's for sure
What he could have become nobody knows
Dead before his time caught up in lyrics of rhythm and rhyme
While seeking still peace sublime
Though still though we shine

Mankind in our time seeking still peace sublime.
Jarrett Watkins

A SACRED PLACE

The body is a warm sacred place

In which a soul is supposed to find solace

And rejoice in the praise of its creator

For in the body the soul can live in this wonderful world

Enjoying the nature of this planet on this plane

In this time

The body is a warm sacred place

ONCE UPON A TIME

Once upon a time a long time ago
There lived a brother that we all should know
They nailed him on a cross our sins to bear
I'm sorry brother I wasn't there
But today my momma say I got your hair
And your style and that smile
She loved the way you drew the crowd wild
With that raw African style
But you left when I was a child
I hear your name today and still I smile

Once upon a time a long time ago
There lived a brother that we all should know
His blood soaked through the wood
Thunder roared from the sky
The son of God was about to die

And now it's been a long time

I'm going to tell a story
I'm going to fill it with my father's glory
Our fathers left a long time ago
And you know a father's absence shows
It's time for fathers to come back home
And reclaim the seats of their thrones
It's time for fathers to come back home
And be loving fathers of their kingdoms

Once upon a time a long time ago
There lived a brother that we all should know

It's time for fathers to come back home and be loving fathers in their kingdoms

I HAD A BROTHER

I had a brother who was stronger than I

I watched him give up the ghost and then die
.
You may sit there with a tear in your eye

And you may cry and wonder why

But one day we all must die

I saw him hold on until the very end

I'm proud to say he was my friend

Death may come in the night

But God's angels will lead you to the light

You may sit there with a tear in your eye

And you may cry and wonder why

But one day we all must die

I had a brother who was stronger than I

BEFORE THE DAYLIGHT

My sister's soul dreams of freedom and flight
Her soul wants to leave in the night
She lies in pain in the hospice room
And we all know death is coming soon

Her once beautiful body and face
Lost forever to cancer's horrid waste
She lies sunken and drained
Cancer spread throughout her body and her brain

We watch helpless in our pain
Her voice faint and hollow
Mary might die tomorrow

Ma'dea told me not to cry
In my angry sadness I asked her why
Why must my sister die
I said she's my sister she's your daughter
If you must force her to drink water
And again I cried while looking at Death
Staring into my eyes
My sister's soul dreams of freedom and flight
Her soul wants to leave before the daylight.

I love you Mary

A PRAYER EVERYDAY

This poem is for you fathers mothers sisters and brothers
Never forget the love we share with one another
Remember that special smile
Even if you haven't seen it in a while
And pass it on down give it to your child

I saw a twinkle in my sister Mary's eyes
Even though she was going to die
I remember how much I cried
Many times I asked God why?
Now I say a special prayer every day
No matter what comes my way
Smile even in pain
Be the day sunny or dark rain
I'm thankful for this life I live
This is my time to give

This poem is for your fathers your mothers your sisters and your brothers
You can do whatever you want to do
I only pray that there is someone you love
And someone who smiles back at you

This poem is for you

RISE UP OUT OF THE ASHES

Rise up out of the ashes
Rise up and let your spirits dream
For we are survivors of vicious schemes
Our fathers awakened from a nightmarish sleep
Found the American Dream never theirs to keep.
Their sins are now ours to bear
Simply because of darkened skin and kinky hair
Degraded in self-hate, ignorant, uneducated
Bombs in our minds activated

So rise up out of the ashes like a Phoenix rises
Allow your minds to reach the skies
To soar like eagles soar
Then listen as lions roar
Listen for they will open doors
As minds explore things you never knew
But they were always a part of you

So rise up out of the ashes for you are God's creation
You are the founding blocks of nations
You come in all sizes shapes colors
We are one we are brothers
All in need of the other
One loving universal mother
Eagles and lions seeking light
No longer fulfilled in darkened nights
Knowledge lips speak to you who listens
As you rise sunlight glistens
With blinding lights of life
Cutting away ignorance like a doctor's knife
Leaving you God's masterpiece to display
I hear your wisdom and I am amazed
For you are my father's child .
Storms are raging but you are mild

And babes shall lead them the Bible says
But first and foremost
You must leave your beds and rise up out of the ashes

HEAL THE WOUND

Today young brothers would murder Jesus
Take back the streets we must

The elder generation must heal the wound heal the cut
Teach a child what not to touch

For how could such a wound bleed
And we not heed our babies' needs
Heal the wound heal the cut
Teach a child what not to touch

Photo by Barry Huber
Ed and Christopher Smith